THE POCKET GUIDE TO
BIRDS OF PREY
OF BRITAIN
AND
NORTHERN EUROPE

GW00672291

THE POCKET GUIDE TO
BIRDS OF PREY
OF BRITAIN
AND
NORTHERN EUROPE

PHILIP BURTON
TREVOR BOYER
Malcolm Ellis
David Thelwell

DRAGON'S
WORLD

Dragon's World Ltd
Limpsfield
Surrey RH8 0DY
Great Britain

First published by Dragon's World 1991.

Editor: Martyn Bramwell
Designer: Tom Deas
Series Design: David Allen
Editorial Director: Pippa Rubinstein

A catalogue record for this book is available from the British Library.

ISBN 1 85028 128 9

Typeset by Flairplan Limited.

Printed in Singapore.

Contents

Introduction 7

Family PANDIONIDAE
OSPREY 19

Family FALCONIDAE
FALCONS 101

Introduction

From the earliest times, birds of prey have occupied a special place in man's feelings towards the natural world. At times his attitudes have appeared favourable, and the aerial hunters have been seen as symbolizing freedom, power and nobility. Conversely, birds of prey have equally often been perceived as a threat, and have been persecuted mercilessly as a result. Neither attitude really does the birds justice, however, and only now are they coming to be valued for their own sake, as superbly adapted living creatures, often endowed with great beauty, and with fascinating ways of life. If this book helps to foster a true appreciation of them, coupled with a concern for their future, then it will have achieved its object.

CLASSIFYING THE BIRDS OF PREY
Hopefully it should be possible to open this book anywhere and find interesting reading coupled with fine illustrations, but in order to understand the birds of prey more fully it is helpful to have a working knowledge of how birds and other living things are classified and named. First of all, terms such as 'birds of prey' and 'raptor' need to be explained. In the broadest sense, any bird that takes animal food, be it the tiniest insect, could be described as a bird of prey, but in practice the term is usually reserved for those that capture prey that is large in proportion to their own size. Usually this will be vertebrate prey – chiefly reptiles, mammals and other birds, but sometimes also fish and amphibians. Even here a difficulty arises because some other groups of birds, such as herons, gulls and crows, take similar animals. All these, however, capture and kill their prey with the bill. True birds of prey have the feet and claws developed into

formidable talons to perform these tasks; in most species the intimidating hooked bill is for tearing up food rather than for killing it in the first place.

Following these criteria then, the term 'birds of prey' is normally understood to include the hawks, eagles, vultures, falcons and allies, and the owls. The first set are grouped together in a single Order called the Falconiformes; these are the day-active birds of prey, also called 'raptors', with which this book is concerned. The owls, the nocturnal birds of prey, are classified in a separate Order, Strigiformes. This implies that the two are not considered to be closely related, and that their similar features have evolved independently. Such judgements about relationships are based on very detailed studies of anatomy, behaviour and biochemistry which try to chart the course taken by evolution. The various levels of grouping therefore aim to reflect ancestry rather than merely overall similarity of features.

Below the level of Order, the next main unit of classification is the Family. Within the Order Falconiformes, five families are recognized – the Cathartidae, Pandionidae, Accipitridae, Sagittariidae and Falconidae. Two of these – the Pandionidae and Sagittariidae – contain just one species each. Surprising as this might seem at first, it is necessary in order to recognize the many unique and fundamental features which set them apart from the larger families.

Continuing down the scale of classification, the next main level of grouping is the Genus, and this leads us into a consideration of nomenclature, as the name of the genus is also the first part of the scientific name of each species. A genus may include only one species if it has no close relatives, or it may include a large number of species. The largest raptor genus, for example, is *Accipiter*, which contains 47 species, all sharing a very similar body plan and way of life. Each species is given a scientific name consisting of the genus name first, followed by the species name; the whole usually being printed in italics. Thus, the Sparrowhawk of Eurasia is called *Accipiter nisus*, while a similar species in North America, the Sharp-shinned Hawk, bears the name *Accipiter striatus*.

The Tawny Eagle (*Aquila rapax*) is an efficient hunter and scavenger, but will also pirate food from other predators.

THE SPECIES ACCOUNTS

In this pocket guide, a standard approach has been taken to the individual species entries. For each species the male bird is illustrated in colour, in full breeding plumage and in a pose characteristic of the bird. On the species distribution maps, tint areas show the year-round range of resident birds and the breeding range of migrants, with solid lines of colour indicating the limits of distribution of migrant birds outside the breeding season.

The concise summary text is presented under a series of headings covering identification features, habitat preferences, nesting habits, food preferences, range, and any known seasonal movements. At the top of each entry there is a data panel giving the bird's average dimensions and weight, and details of the clutch size, eggs, and incubation and fledging periods. Size information is not complete for all species, but in accordance with current widespread practice two dimensions are given wherever possible. Length is that of the bird on its back, from bill tip to tail tip, a condition normally only attainable with a dead specimen. As it is prone to subjective error in measuring it is not available for all species, but it does give some indication of general size. The other measure, wing length, is widely used in ornithology due to its greater precision. It refers to the distance from the wrist joint of the wing to the tip of the longest flight feather. Wing length should not be confused with wing-span, which is the distance between the two wing tips when the wings are fully stretched out. This is the measurement most people are interested in, but unfortunately it is even more prone to error than body length, and is consequently available only for a small proportion of species. Accordingly it has been omitted here, but as a rough guide, the span of many large soaring birds of prey is about three times the wing length.

Individuals vary in size in all species, but where this variation is not large, a single median value is given. For many species, however, it is necessary to give a size range. This may be due to geographical variation, but more usually it is due to the size difference between the sexes. Interestingly, in most birds of prey it is the female that is the larger, and the difference is most marked in many bird-eating species. It is least marked in scavenging species, and in some vultures particularly, the males are somewhat larger, as in the majority of birds. It has been suggested that the usual greater size

The Lanner Falcon (*Falco biarmicus*) is the only falcon known to take its prey head-on, a feat requiring exceptional timing and flying agility.

of females is necessary to enable them to establish the dominance that causes the males to bring food throughout incubation and much of the fledging period. The size difference may also have some safety value during courtship, so strong are the aggressive urges of the male.

THE FLIGHT CHARACTERISTICS OF RAPTORS

Much interest is shown in the powers of flight displayed by birds of prey, although there is often some misunderstanding on this topic. High speed, as demonstrated by falcons such as the Peregrine, for example, is not by any means a universal characteristic of raptors; indeed some are actually specialized for flying extremely slowly. Taking the group as a whole, the range of wing shape and mode of flight is very wide indeed. In comparing them, key factors to be considered are wing loading, aspect ratio, and the shape of the primaries or main flight feathers.

Wing loading is a simple enough concept; it is simply the relationship between body weight and wing area. Birds that have a large wing area relative to their weight are said to have low wing loading, and vice versa. Among birds of prey, harriers have the lowest wing loading at some 2 to 3 kilogrammes per square metre. Unspecialized birds of prey such as buzzards stand at around 4 to 4.5 kg per square metre; sparrowhawks and goshawks at about 5.5 kg per square metre, and large falcons at about 7 kg per square metre. In general, higher wing loadings are associated with more rapid flight, and this is especially true for birds such as falcons, which attain maximum speed in a dive. Highest loadings of all, however, are found in large eagles and vultures. Although their huge wings have a very large

area, their bodies are proportionately heavier still, and wing loading can be as high as 12 kg per square metre. The very low wing loading of harriers is related to their method of hunting, which involves quartering a stretch of ground very slowly and systematically. As they do this they are not only looking for prey but also listening for it, as hearing is especially highly developed in this group.

Aspect ratio is the ratio of wing length to wing breadth. Short, broad wings have low aspect ratios; long narrow ones have high aspect ratios. High aspect ratios are most suited to soaring and gliding, but in their most extreme form, as in albatrosses, they make take-off slow and difficult and cause proportionately more turbulence, so that a high air-speed is required. Soaring raptors such as vultures and some eagles have wings a good deal broader than this to permit slower flight with greater manoeuvreability. Very low aspect ratios are typical of forest species, which may have to weave in and out of trees at high speed as they pursue their prey.

The shape and relative length of the primary flight feathers affects the whole appearance and functioning of the wing tip. Swift species such as the falcons have pointed wing tips, but in many species the shape is more rounded, and the feathers themselves may have a 'cut-away' outline so that their tips appear widely separated, like splayed fingers. Particularly strongly marked in large soaring species, this feature helps smooth the air flow over the wing, a vital factor when air-speed is slow. The 'alula', a bunch of feathers attached to the vestigial thumb of the wing skeleton, has a similar effect, and functions rather like the flaps that are deployed as an aircraft comes in to land.

Soaring species, when not migrating, are generally using their high vantage-point to look for ground-living prey or carrion. The same is generally true for those species that 'still hunt', that is, watch for prey from a perch. Raptors that take their prey in flight have attracted particular interest, however, and careful studies of falconers' birds using high-speed cinematography have clarified the technique they employ. It is the large falcons and the accipiters (sparrowhawks and goshawks) that specialize most in this type of hunting, falcons typically attacking in a dive or 'stoop', while accipiters generally attack in level flight. Both, especially the falcons, are travelling very fast when they overtake their prey, but this speed is primarily concerned with bringing them into a killing position. What then happens is that the pelvis and legs are swung at the prey, adding greatly to the force of the blow. Peregrines in fact level out and slow down somewhat as they strike, and in any case deliver only a glancing blow with the open feet. This is still enough to cause instant death in most cases: were the strike any harder, the falcon would endanger its own limbs, to no good purpose. I have so far avoided being struck by a raptor, but have twice been the target for a Tawny Owl, which uses a similar technique. Such a blow feels like a direct hit from a brick, and one is astonished that it can have come from a bird weighing no more than about half a kilogramme.

THREATS TO THE BIRDS OF PREY

Concern over environmental issues is now a prominent feature of current affairs, and birds of prey illustrate very clearly some of the key problems in conservation. The relationship between the numbers of prey and the number of predators is one of the most crucial of these. One of the chief reasons why birds of prey have so often been persecuted is their supposed depletion of stocks of game. This ignores the fact that under natural conditions it is the numbers of prey that control the numbers of predators, and not the other way about. Thus, if two grouse moors of equal size are hunted respectively by one pair of eagles and by two pairs, it can be confidently predicted that the moor with the extra eagles has substantially more grouse on it, not less. The only exceptions to this occur when numbers of predators are maintained at an artificially high level by some human activity such as the disposal of offal or garbage, which provides a large supplementary food source. This type of problem occurs more commonly with such predators as gulls than with raptors.

Birds of prey are, indeed, much less numerous than most of the smaller species they feed on, but because they are relatively large and conspicuous this fact is often overlooked. It does, however, make them much more vulnerable to persecution or environmental hazards. Where pollutants are concerned, an additional problem is that although the chemicals are initially widely dispersed, they accumulate in ever greater concentrations as they move upward through a food pyramid, and birds of prey which generally stand at the top of such pyramids may receive them in dangerous concentrations. For this reason, birds of prey can serve as valuable indicators of the health of our environment, and studies of their breeding success and ecology play a prominent role in monitoring the impact of modern technology on the world we live in.

BOYER

Persecution and the use of
pesticides have greatly
reduced the number of
White-tailed Sea Eagles
(*Haliaeetus albicilla*) in
Europe, and this
magnificent bird is now
numerous only in Norway.

OSPREY

Family PANDIONIDAE

Osprey
Pandion haliaetus

Length:	56cm	**Eggs:**	3 (2-4), white, marked with brown and grey
Wing:	482mm		
Weight:	1120-2050g	**Incubation:**	32-33 days
		Fledging:	50-60 days

Identification: The male Osprey has a white head, a dark brown crown and broad, blackish eye-stripe; otherwise the plumage is deep brown above, white below. The eye is pale yellow, with legs and feet greenish white. The female is similar, but has an upper breast band of brown streaks.

Habitat: The most usual place to find Ospreys is near large lakes and rivers, or the sea. The presence of large trees, or rocky outcrops, on which the birds can perch between hunting forays, seems to be an added requirement.

Nest: The nest is a large, rather untidy, grass-lined structure made of sticks, which the birds snap off trees by grasping them with the feet as they fly past. It is usually sited on top of a tree or crag, and sometimes even on a telegraph pole. Increasingly, the birds are building on pole-mounted platforms erected specially for them. The nest is used, and added to, for many years, and may become as large as 1.5 metres in diameter, and almost as high.

Food: Although items such as crustaceans and birds occasionally figure in the Osprey's diet, its food consists almost entirely of fish, weighing up to 1.8 kg, which it captures in spectacular fashion. The bird hovers, up to 30 metres above the water, then plunge-dives, feet first, onto its prey, often becoming almost totally submerged. The fish is then carried off, held head-forward in the feet, which are positioned one behind the other.

Range: Worldwide, the Osprey's range is one of the largest of any raptor. In Europe, it nests principally in Scandinavia and Eastern Europe, with scattered smaller groups around the Mediterranean. Recolonized after a long absence, Scotland now has a healthy and growing population of Ospreys.

Movements: The species migrates south to winter mainly in Africa south of the Sahara.

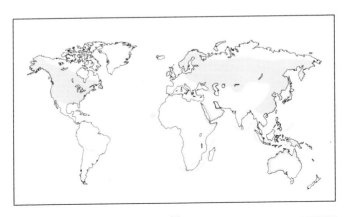

Kites, Vultures Eagles and Hawks

Family Accipitridae

Honey Buzzard

Pernis apivorus

Length:	51-58cm	**Eggs:**	2, whitish with rich red-brown freckling	
Wing:	375-425mm	**Incubation:**	30-35 days	
Weight:	440-1050g	**Fledging:**	40-44 days	

Identification: Highly variable in plumage, the relatively small head aids distinction from the Common Buzzard whether flying or perched. Overhead, the tail appears relatively longer. The wings show several narrow dark bars, and the tail has two narrow bars near the base and a broader one at the tip.

Habitat: Breeding habitat is woodland, mainly deciduous, either large forests with clearings or smaller woods where the bird can hunt at the edges. Wooded savanna or open forest are frequented in the winter quarters.

T.BOYER

Nest: A stick nest is built, often with the old nest of another bird as a foundation, and sited 15 to 20 metres up in a forest tree. The nest varies in size, being usually smaller than the Common Buzzard's, but it is always lined with plentiful sprays of fresh greenery. In use, the nest and its surroundings quickly become littered with pieces of wasps' nests.

Food: Mainly the nests of wasps and bees, together with their contents of grubs, adults and honey. These are apparently located in flight, and it is possible the bird follows wasps for long distances to track them back to their nests. Honey Buzzards move easily on the ground, either walking or running as they manoeuvre around a wasps' nest, and the feet are used to dig into it. Adult insects are seized out of the air and the sting nipped off before they are swallowed. Their attacks are disregarded; the short stiff feathers of the face give the bird some protection. Small mammals, reptiles and frogs are also taken, as well as some non-venomous insects.

Range: Honey Buzzards breed throughout Europe and Asia from 63°N southwards. In Britain, they are summer visitors in small numbers to southern counties.

Movements: Northern populations are highly migratory; southern ones more sedentary. The passage of large numbers of Honey Buzzards is one of the spectacular features of autumn passage at narrow straits such as Falsterbo in southern Sweden, Gibraltar and the Bosphorus. Maximum numbers passing are estimated at 126,000 over Gibraltar and 26,000 at the Bosphorus.

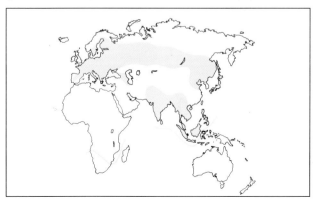

Black-shouldered Kite

Elanus caeruleus

Length:	33cm	**Eggs:**	3-4, creamy, with dark brown blotches and smears
Wing:	280mm	**Incubation:**	25-28 days
Weight:	c.230g	**Fledging:**	30-35 days

Identification: Unmistakable, with its elegant grey and white plumage and black shoulder patch. Hovering is a regular method of hunting, so a distant view in poor light might lead to confusion with the Common Kestrel, but the tail is shorter and the wing tips more rounded. Its method of descending onto prey is also highly characteristic; rather than diving with half-closed wings like a falcon, it raises the wings vertically above the back and drops like a stone.

Habitat: Arid, open areas ranging from semi-desert and savanna to open cultivated areas. Though frequenting essentially dry country, some nearby water is preferred.

Nest: A frail platform of twigs, sometimes with a little dry grass. It is placed in an isolated tree, often a thorny one, from 2 to 10 metres up.

Food: Small mammals up to young rat size are the chief diet, varied with some ground-living small birds such as larks. Some reptiles are also taken and in places large insects such as locusts. Early morning is a favoured time for hunting, either by watching from a perch, or by flying slowly about with frequent bouts of hovering. Some prey is consumed on the wing.

Range: The Black-shouldered Kite is found throughout the warmer areas of the Old World, and is replaced by two closely related species in Australia. In Europe it is confined to a few scattered localities in Spain and Portugal.

Movements: Basically a sedentary species, but individuals have wandered to Holland, Belgium, Germany and France.

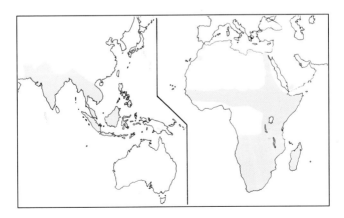

Black Kite
Milvus migrans

Length:	56cm	**Eggs:**	2-5, white, spotted with red-brown
Wing:	417-465mm	**Incubation:**	38 days
Weight:	630-1030g	**Fledging:**	40-42 days

Identification: Darker and duller colouring, and a less deeply forked tail distinguish the Black Kite from the Red. The long tail with its shallow notch, and relatively narrower wings separate it from the buzzards (*Buteo*).

Habitat: Typical breeding habitat in Europe is forest margin beside lakes or rivers, but nests are sometimes several kilometres from water. Outside the breeding season, lakes and rivers are still favoured, and Black Kites will forage freely in cities or on rubbish dumps where there are good opportunities for scavenging.

Nest: Usually placed in a tree, less commonly on a building or cliff, the nest is a stick platform about 0.5 metres across, with a deep cup in the middle. It is generally 'decorated' not with green leaves, as in many other raptors, but with bits of refuse such as rags, paper and other garbage. Between 8 and 15 metres is the usual height range, but some may be sited over 30 metres above the ground. Generally a solitary breeder, the Black Kite may nest colonially in places.

Food: A master scavenger, this great opportunist can display remarkable aerial agility in snatching food. Unable to kill prey much larger than a rat, it also gleans all kinds of carrion and scraps, and has a fondness for fish. Live prey taken includes many young birds such as ducks, moorhens and gulls. Amphibians and reptiles are taken, as well as insects, worms and snails; some insects are captured in flight.

Range: With a distribution covering much of the Old World, the Black Kite ranks as one of the world's most successful raptors, probably due to its ability to exploit man's activities. However, the species is gradually declining. Improved hygiene in cities, especially in Europe, has reduced some of its scavenging opportunities, but pesticide poisoning has probably also been an important factor.

Movements: Northern breeding birds (including virtually all European breeders) are migratory, passing across Gibraltar and the Bosphorus on their way to Africa south of the Sahara. Maximum autumn totals of 40,000 at Gibraltar and 2700 at the Bosphorus have been recorded.

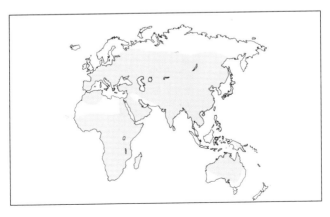

Red Kite
Milvus milvus

Length:	61cm	**Eggs:**	2-4, white, with purplish or reddish-brown markings
Wing:	480-515mm	**Incubation:**	28-30 days
Weight:	750-1380g	**Fledging:**	45-50 days

Identification: Paler, more rufous plumage, and a very long deeply forked reddish tail should preclude confusion with the Black Kite. From below, the wings show a conspicuous pale patch in the outer half, while seen from above, a pale band extends along the wing coverts. Black Kites, especially young

T. BOYER

birds, show similar patterning, but are much duller and less striking.

Habitat: Wooded, hilly or mountainous country. The presence of water is less necessary than for the Black Kite.

Nest: Sited at a height of 10 to 30 metres, the nest of sticks is usually built on top of the old nest of another bird such as a buzzard or Raven. Oaks, beeches and firs are favoured trees. Rags or other bits of rubbish are also included.

Food: Foraging Red Kites sail about low over meadows or other open ground with graceful buoyant flight, and agile manoeuvring, in which the tail twists about and changes shape. The Red Kite takes more live prey than the Black Kite, including rodents, young hares, young birds, frogs, lizards and insects. Red Kites take fewer stranded fish than Black Kites, but will readily feed on carrion where available. In some areas they frequent main roads, looking for traffic casualties.

Range: North and East Europe, scattered localities around the Mediterranean, the Iberian Peninsula and Wales. A distinct race occurs on the Cape Verde Islands. Always less widely distributed than the Black Kite, its decline in numbers has been much more marked, due to more intensive persecution.

Movements: Northern breeders are migratory, some travelling as far as North Africa. Others are more sedentary, but even birds of the Welsh population may move into England in winter, and continental ringed individuals have occasionally turned up in Wales.

African Fish Eagle
Haliaeetus vocifer

Length:	63-73cm	**Eggs:**	1-3, white, sometimes with faint spots
Wing:	510-605mm		
Weight ♂:	1900-2500g	**Incubation:**	44-45 days
Weight ♀:	3200-3600g	**Fledging:**	65-75 days

Identification: Similar in proportion to the sea eagles, but smaller. Adults are unmistakable, with white head and breast and white tail contrasting with chestnut plumage and black flight feathers. Young birds are a more nondescript mottled brown, but may be recognized by the off-white nape and eyebrow, and whitish tail with a dark terminal band. African Fish Eagles are noisy birds, frequently uttering clear piercing calls, which once heard are never forgotten, and are as good a recognition feature as any plumage characteristics.

Habitat: Lakes, rivers, wetlands and wooded sea coasts.

Nest: Trees are the usual site, though a cliff, low bush or even the ground may be used where they are lacking. Euphorbias, thorny acacias and figs are commonly selected. The nest itself is made of sticks, and well lined with papyrus heads, grass and leaves, and, curiously, weaver bird nests. One to three nests are maintained by a pair, and these are used roughly in rotation from year to year.

Food: Predominantly fish, catfish and lungfish being especially favoured. Short flights out from a perch are the usual hunting method, longer soaring forays being undertaken if these do not reveal prey. African Fish Eagles also capture both young and adults of various water birds, especially Lesser Flamingos.

Range: The greater part of Africa south of the Sahara.

Movements: Though not a migratory species, young birds wander, and three individuals have been recorded from Egypt.

Pallas's Sea Eagle
Haliaeetus leucoryphus

Length:	76-84cm	**Eggs:**	2-4, dull white
Wing:	545-598mm	**Incubation:**	40 days
Weight:	2000-3700g	**Fledging:**	70-105 days

Identification: Long but relatively narrow wings, long tail and long head and neck give a quite different outline from the White-tailed Sea Eagle, when only the silhouette can be

discerned. With better views, the adult's pale head, rufous upper breast and black tail with a broad white band are diagnostic. Juveniles may present more difficulty as they are largely dark brown, but seen overhead, helpful features are a pale patch near the wing tip, and a pale line along the middle of the wing.

Habitat: Typically large inland lakes, rivers and wetlands of Central Asia, sometimes up to altitudes of 4000-5000 metres. Wintering birds may appear on sea coasts in some places, such as the Crimea. Wanderers in Western Europe have occasionally turned up at lakes and reservoirs.

Nest: Tree sites are used where available, but in their absence the nest may be placed on a cliff or even on the ground, on a sand bank or in a reed bed. A large structure of sticks and reeds, lined with sparse grass and greenery, it may be less than 0.5 metres thick when new, but added to year after year it may reach a depth of 2 metres.

Food: Fish and water birds make up much of its diet, some taken in the form of carrion, others young or disabled; it appears to capture relatively little fully active prey. Frogs, snakes and tortoises are also recorded. Pallas' Sea Eagles may congregate around places where fishing boats land, and will harry Ospreys to rob them of fish.

Range: Breeds in Central Asia, from Kirghizia to Manchuria, and south to northern India.

Movements: Winters west to the Crimea and Iraq, and south to India. Stragglers, invariably young birds, have wandered west to Finland, Poland, Norway and France.

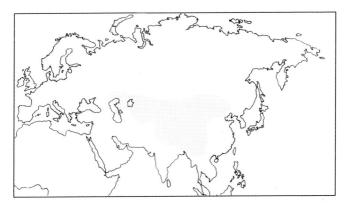

White-tailed Sea Eagle
Haliaeetus albicilla

Length:	69-91cm	**Eggs:**	1-3, dull white
Wing:	559-711mm	**Incubation:**	38-42 days
Weight ♂:	3100-5400g	**Fledging:**	70-80 days
Weight ♀:	4100-6900g		

Identification: Long, very broad wings, their front and back edges parallel, short tail and the head projecting very far forwards, lend this species a distinctive silhouette which should prevent confusion with other large eagles. Adults have a dull brown body with pale head and white tail; juveniles are darker, and have brown tails.

Habitat: Sea coasts in the northern part of the range, large lakes and rivers elsewhere.

. BOYER

Nest: The birds prefer to build their huge nest in a large tree, usually more than 18 metres above the ground, but where no trees are available they will select a rocky crag, or even a low hummock. The birds have several alternative nests, which may be added to at any time, and which, after several years, can become huge structures of branches and twigs measuring 2 metres across by 3 metres deep. The deep central cup is lined with greenery, and sometimes wool.

Food: Prey is sought either from a perch, or while circling about 200-300 metres up. Fish may constitute up to 90 per cent of the diet, supplemented by some mammals and birds and carrion, the latter mainly in winter. Fish are snatched from the surface after a low level approach, rather than a plunge like that of the Osprey. Diving birds may be attacked repeatedly until too exhausted to continue submerging.

Range: From Greenland right across northern and north-central Asia. In Europe it is now largely confined to Scandinavia and the East. Formerly breeding around the coasts of Scotland, Ireland and western England, it was exterminated by persecution by the turn of the century. A programme of reintroduction in western Scotland is now achieving encouraging success.

Movements: Adult birds are sedentary except in northern Russia, but young White-tailed Sea Eagles are more mobile and may wander extensively, some reaching southern Europe and England. A bird ringed as a nestling in Germany was recovered in Norfolk in 1985.

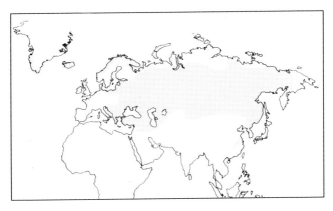

Egyptian Vulture
Neophron percnopterus

Length:	58-66cm	**Eggs:**	2, white blotched with brown
Wing:	470-530mm	**Incubation:**	42 days
Weight:	2000-2400g	**Fledging:**	70-90 days

Identification: Characteristic vulture flight-silhouette with long broad wings and short tail, allied to white colour contrasting with black flight feathers make adults unmistakable. White Storks have the same colour pattern, but only when so far off that the long trailing legs are invisible could a stork be mistaken for a vulture. Young birds are dark brown, gradually acquiring the white plumage over four years. They can still be distinguished from other vultures by their generally smaller size, thin pointed bill and wedge-shaped tail.
Habitat: Open country, ranging from rocky hills and cultivated land to savannas and semi-desert. Egyptian Vultures

T. BOYER

will also scavenge in towns and villages squalid enough to provide plenty of carrion and garbage scraps.

Nests are often, but by no means invariably, close to rivers.

Nest: A crevice or small cave on a cliff is the preferred situation in which to build the relatively small nest of sticks. The same site is likely to be used year after year. Trees or buildings are occasionally used where suitable cliff holes are lacking.

Food: Egyptian Vultures take carrion and garbage from the smallest scraps up to pieces of large carcasses. At the latter, they are subordinate to the larger vultures, but secure scraps by opportunistic snatching, or where the narrower bill enables them to reach portions that are inaccessible to the others. Fond of eggs of any kind, it gains access to Ostrich eggs by throwing stones at them with the bill. Live prey consists only of insects, some collected while following the plough.

Range: Southern Europe, the Middle East, India and Africa. It is declining in Europe, due to reduction in food supply resulting from improved human hygiene, and to some persecution.

Movements: The European population is migratory, wintering in Africa south of the Sahara, where the birds mingle with resident populations. Young birds may remain there for a year or two, returning to Europe when mature. Migrants travel by soaring, and cross the Mediterranean at Gibraltar and the Bosphorus. Numbers passing at the former in autumn may reach 6000 while 500 is about the limit at the latter.

Lammergeier

Gypaetus barbatus

Length:	102-114cm	**Eggs:**	1-2, pale rufous with dark mottling
Wing:	762-914mm	**Incubation:**	53 days
Weight:	1220-1900g	**Fledging:**	107-117 days

Identification: Long narrow wings and long pointed tail give the Lammergeier a flight outline like no other raptor. Seen perched, the Lammergeier's pale head with black 'beard' is conspicuous at a considerable distance.

Habitat: Confined to mountain ranges, occurring up to high altitudes, and rarely wandering to low-lying areas.

Nest: Placed in a sheltered cliff ledge or cave, the nest is a broad, flat stick structure that may exceed 2 metres in width. The lining includes wool, dung and rubbish, and much food refuse such as bones and horns.

Food: Carrion and offal of all kinds are taken, including occasional human corpses. Although dominated at a carcass by Black or Griffon vultures, the Lammergeier is more capable of raptorial behaviour than most vultures. It is the only one that regularly carries food in its talons. Although this is usually picked up dead, there are records of live prey such as monitor lizards being seized in this way. Many accounts mention the bird trying to force large animals such as goats, chamois and even people over precipices, and there could be some truth in these. Better substantiated is its habit of dropping bones from a height to break them open. By doing this, it gains access to the marrow, which it is able to extract with its stiff gouge-shaped tongue.

Range: Mountainous areas from southern Europe through much of Asia and Africa. Its numbers have declined seriously in Europe, where efforts are being made to re-establish it in the Alps.

Movements: The Lammergeier is not migratory.

Hooded Vulture

Necrosyrtes monachus

Length: 57-62cm
Wing: 470mm
Weight: 1524-2102g

Eggs: 1, white with red-brown blotches
Incubation: 46 days
Fledging: 120 days

Identification: A small vulture, with thin bill and dark brown colouration, this species could only be confused with an immature Egyptian Vulture. The square-ended rather than wedge-shaped tail serves to distinguish it.

Habitat: Principally a bird of savannas, the Hooded Vulture is also found in forested country around towns and villages, and more rarely in desert areas.

Nest: Usually in trees, especially baobabs and silk-cotton trees, but sometimes on cliffs. Placed anywhere from 6 to 35 metres above the ground, the nest is rather less than a metre wide and deep. It is made of sticks, lined with grass, green leaves and bits of rubbish. Fresh leaves are added from time to time while nesting is in progress. The nest is refurbished and re-used year after year.

Food: All kinds of carrion and garbage, and insects such as termites and locusts. A tame species, it will wander around market places to scavenge, or amongst people working in fields to find grubs in newly turned soil. At a large carcass it is dominated by larger species, but obtains small scraps by opportunism.

Range: The greater part of Africa south of the Sahara, occasionally wandering to North Africa.

Movements: Young birds may wander, but this is not generally a migratory species.

Indian White-backed Vulture
Gyps bengalensis

Length:	c.90cm	**Eggs:**	1, dull white
Wing:	560mm	**Incubation:**	45-52 days
Weight:	not recorded	**Fledging:**	c.90 days

Identification: Birds of all ages show a conspicuous white bar on the underside of the wing; adults are also easily recognized by the white back. Seen close to, the short, deep bill is characteristic.

Habitat: Cultivated or wooded country, but not forests or deserts.

Nest: Colonial. Nests are placed 10 to 18 metres up, typically in a banyan, mango or casuarina tree near a village or road. They are large stick platforms, many of the branches with green leaves still attached. The central depression is lined with green leaves, wool, dung and rubbish.

Food: Carrion, the birds often congregating in numbers at large carcasses.

Range: India to Burma and Vietnam. The Indian White-backed Vulture has benefited from expanding cultivation, and its numbers are increasing.

Movements: A migrant to Afghanistan in summer, this species has wandered to the Near East.

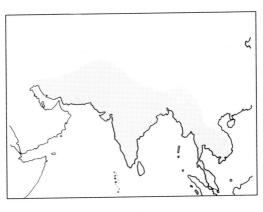

Rüppell's Griffon

Gyps rueppellii

Length: 102cm   **Eggs:** 1-2, white tinged greenish
Wing: 635mm   **Incubation:** not recorded
Weight: 7710-9000g   **Fledging:** not recorded

Identification: Adults on the ground are easily identified by the scaly patterning of the upperparts. Young are uniform dark brown, and similar to young of the African White-backed Vulture, *Gyps africanus*, but larger and paler.

Habitat: Dry plains and deserts, often mountainous regions or savanna areas which can be reached from mountains or rock outcrops. The birds roost on inaccessible cliff faces, some individuals returning regularly to the same ledge.

Nest: Colonial, nesting on crags in groups of up to 100 pairs. Built by both sexes, the nests are made of sticks, and are not very substantial, sometimes being smaller than the incubating bird itself. Green leaves and grass are added as a lining.

Food: Carrion, often fresh, as the species is quick to locate new food sources. It gathers in large jostling mobs at a carcass, some birds getting right inside. Its main competitor at carcasses is the White-backed Vulture; being a more powerful bird it usually prevails, though the Lappet-faced Vulture if present dominates both. The cliff face roosts are sometimes far from the foraging areas, occasionally as much as 150 km, the birds travelling to them at great height, using thermals. Rüppell's Griffon holds the avian height record of 37,000 feet, one having been killed by an aircraft at that altitude.

Range: Central, Eastern and northeast Africa.

Movements: This species is not migratory.

Griffon Vulture
Gyps fulvus

Length: 97-104cm   **Eggs:** 1, white
Wing: 690-750mm   **Incubation:** 48-54 days
Weight: 6200-11000g   **Fledging:** 110-115 days

Identification: Only likely to be confused with the Black Vulture in Europe, and then only when colour cannot be seen. Its flight silhouette is different, however, with a markedly more curved outline to the rear edge of the wings. Also, it soars with its wings raised at a slight dihedral, whereas the Black Vulture holds them flat.

Habitat: Typically a bird of mountainous areas, especially when breeding, but visits plains areas to forage.

Nest: Colonial, nesting on cliffs in groups of 5 to 100 pairs. The nests are rather flat stick structures, lined with green leaves, generally less than a metre in diameter. New material is added throughout the nesting cycle.

Food: Carrion, usually the carcasses of medium to large animals, but also some dead birds and fish, as well as the afterbirth of sheep.

Range: From southern Europe, through Central Asia, south to northern India. The species is decreasing, especially in Europe, where rising standards of hygiene have greatly reduced its food supplies. About 6000 pairs are estimated to breed in the Western Palearctic.

Movements: Adults are not migratory, but young birds wander and some migrate, passing over narrow straits such as Gibraltar and the Bosphorus.

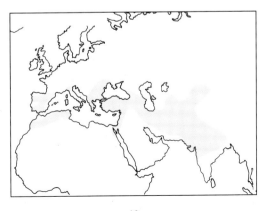

Lappet-faced Vulture

Torgos tracheliotus

Length:	99-102cm	**Eggs:**	1, white, blotched brown
Wing:	715-795mm	**Incubation:**	c.55 days
Weight:	6350-6800g	**Fledging:**	c.125 days

T. BOYER

Identification: Africa's largest vulture. At close range the adult's pink or red wattled head renders it unmistakable, and even the duller immatures are easily recognized by their massive deep bills. In flight, its similar outline could lead to confusion with the European Black Vulture in the few places where the two may overlap. Distinguishing features are two pale bands along the underside of the wing, paler wing coverts above, and (in the adult) white thigh patches.

Habitat: Arid plains, thornbush and deserts.

Nest: Typically a huge, flat stick structure on top of a flat acacia thorn tree. In treeless areas it nests on cliffs. The nest may exceed 2 metres in width, and has a central cup lined with fur, dung and grass.

Food: Mainly carrion, though it also kills small mammals and birds, and takes some insects. It will take both adult and young flamingos at colonies, as well as eating their eggs. At a carcass it dominates smaller species, and with its heavy bill is sometimes the only one capable of opening it up.

Range: Dry areas throughout Africa. A few pairs also breed in Israel.

Movements: Not migratory, but young birds may wander considerable distances. There is a nineteenth century record of one from the French Pyrenees.

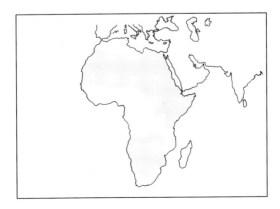

European Black Vulture

Aegypius monachus

Length:	99-107cm	**Eggs:**	1, white, with red-brown or purplish markings, often dense	
Wing:	715-840mm	**Incubation:**	52-55 days	
Weight:	7000-12500g	**Fledging:**	100-120 days	

Identification: Huge; on average the largest Old World vulture, though there is some overlap with the Lappet-faced Vulture. The overall dark colour and greyish head skin with black down are characteristic. In flight, the rear edge of the

wings appears nearly parallel with the front, unlike the Griffon, and it soars with the wings flat, or even slightly drooped when gliding. Darker and more uniform wings, both above and below, separate it from the Lappet-faced Vulture.

Habitat: Mountainous areas in Europe, but also flat, semi-desert areas in Asia.

Nest: An enormous structure, which is added to over the years, becoming up to 2 metres wide, and as many deep. Though cliff ledges are sometimes used, it is generally sited in a tree, often one on a slope, where rising air currents aid the bird's flight. The nest is made of sticks, with leaves and conifer shoots, pieces of bark and skin from carcasses.

Food: Chiefly carrion, though small mammals up to the size of hares are occasionally taken. The bird apparently regularly takes tortoises in India, its powerful bill enabling it to wrench meat from inside the carapace. Dominating other vultures, including Griffons at a carcass, it can afford to turn up late and force them aside. On other occasions, it may be the only one capable of opening up the corpse.

Range: In Europe it breeds in mainland Spain and Majorca, with a few more in the Balkans. In Asia, it occurs across Anatolia and onwards through Central Asia. The European population has declined seriously due to reduction of food supplies and persecution, and is currently estimated at somewhat over 200 pairs.

Movements: European birds are not migratory, but Asian ones move south in winter to the Red Sea, northern India and Burma.

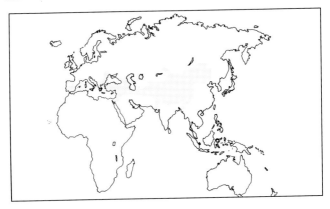

Short-toed Eagle

Circaetus gallicus

Length:	63-69cm	**Eggs:**	1, white
Wing:	510-605mm	**Incubation:**	47 days
Weight ♂:	1180-2000g	**Fledging:**	70-75 days (Europe)
Weight ♀:	1303-2324g		90 days (Africa)

Identification: Dark head and upper breast contrasting with generally very pale underparts are characteristic of this medium-sized eagle. The wings are long and broad, and the head outline broad and rounded. Some Common Buzzards

T. BOYER

and Honey Buzzards may have similar colouring, but are shorter-winged and narrower-headed. A further useful point is that this species usually soars with the wings distinctly raised upwards.

Habitat: Dry, open country, or scattered woodland, with some preference for undulating hilly ground. Highly cultivated areas are avoided.

Nest: A relatively flimsy stick structure, less than a metre across, with a deep central cup lined with green leaves or pine sprays. Sited on top of low trees, sometimes as little as 3 metres up, they are nevertheless difficult to see because they are usually well screened by foliage. Rarely, nests may be sited on rock ledges. Nests may be re-used, but not always in successive years.

Food: This is the only snake eagle breeding in Europe, and snakes do indeed form about 95 per cent of its diet. The rest is mainly lizards, with occasional mammals up to rabbit size. Short, rough-soled toes enable it to grip snakes firmly. After capturing a snake, the bird quickly kills it by attacking its head with the bill, and then swallows it whole unless it is very large. Snakes are swallowed head first, sometimes in flight.

Range: Southern Europe, the Middle East, Central Asia and Africa.

Movements: Northern breeders migrate south in winter. European birds, moving to Africa in autumn, pass over Gibraltar and the Bosphorus. Maximum autumn counts are over 2000 at the former and 9000 at the latter.

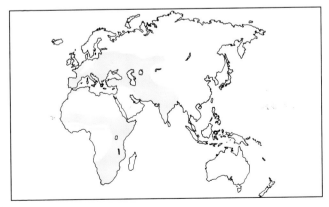

Bateleur

Terathopius ecaudatus

Length:	61cm	**Eggs:**	1, chalky white
Wing:	482-533mm	**Incubation:**	42-43 days
Weight:	1927-2950g	**Fledging:**	90-125 days

Identification: Whether in handsome adult plumage or dull immature feathering, the Bateleur can immediately be recognized by the combination of an extremely short tail and very long wings. Perched, the wing tips extend far beyond the tail, while the flight outline is like no other raptor. The bird gets its name from the French word for acrobat, referring to its continual side to side tilting action as it glides at high speed.

Habitat: Savannas and thornbush country.

Nest: A compact stick structure, lined with green leaves, the nest is usually sited in an acacia tree, 3 to 10 metres up. It is used year after year, gradually increasing in bulk. Bateleurs are curious among birds of prey in frequently having a third adult, usually a male, present at the nest throughout the breeding cycle.

Food: Primarily a snake eater, the Bateleur also consumes a wide range of other prey. Various small mammals, a few ground birds, lizards, tortoises and even fish are recorded. The snakes taken include a number of venomous species, including even the deadly Puff Adder.

Range: Suitable country throughout Africa south of the Sahara.

Movements: Not migratory, but occasionally birds wander as far as Arabia and North Africa.

Marsh Harrier
Circus aeruginosus

Length:	51cm	**Eggs:**	3-8, bluish white
Wing:	381-432mm	**Incubation:**	33-38 days
Weight ♂:	405-667g	**Fledging:**	35-42 days
Weight ♀:	540-800g		

Identification: Harriers are long-winged, long-tailed raptors with slow, buoyant flight, usually at low altitude. The Marsh Harrier is the largest, and easily distinguished from the others by its generally dark coloration. Males have paler grey on wings and tail, varying in amount. However, even the palest males can still be recognized by the dark belly.

Habitat: As its name indicates, this is primarily a marshland species, normally foraging and breeding in reed beds. It will also venture out into land adjoining marshes, and is sometimes to be seen quartering low over a cornfield.

Nest: Placed on the ground amongst reeds, or sometimes crops, the nest is a thick platform of sticks, reeds and grass. The main nest is built by the female, but the male also constructs false nests which are used as feeding platforms.

Food: Marsh-dwelling creatures of many kinds. Small mammals are a major item, but the bird also takes frogs, snakes, lizards and young waterbirds. Adult Coots and Moorhens are also captured. Some fish are eaten, but whether picked up live or stranded is not clear.

Range: In suitable habitat throughout most of the Old World, including Australia.

Movements: Northern and eastern populations migrate to the Mediterranean area and Africa south of the Sahara. Harriers travel on a broad front, and do not concentrate in great numbers at narrow straits like many raptors.

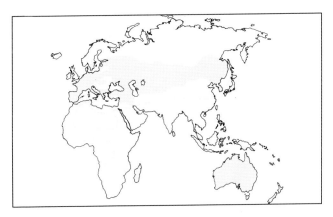

Hen Harrier

Circus cyaneus

Length:	43-51cm	**Eggs:**	5 (4-6), bluish white,
Wing:	333-406mm		sometimes brown blotched
Weight ♂:	300-400g	**Incubation:**	29-39 days
Weight ♀:	410-708g	**Fledging:**	35-40 days

T. BOYER

Identification: With his soft pearl-grey plumage, contrasting black primaries, and white rump and underparts, the male Hen Harrier is a stunningly beautiful bird. The female is duller, with a brown back, and similarly coloured spots and streaks on the underside, although she, too, has a white rump.

Habitat: Although found in many habitats, the Hen Harrier seems to prefer low-lying wetlands, open fields and young conifer plantations.

Nest: The nest, usually in a hollow protected by vegetation, is made of small sticks, and various reeds and grasses. It varies in diameter from about 40cm in dry situations to up to 1 metre, and may be 10 to 20cm deep in wet locations.

Food: The species preys mainly on small songbirds and their fledglings, voles, leverets and young rabbits, but it will also take frogs, small reptiles and some insects.

Range: The Hen Harrier is distributed patchily across much of northern Europe, though populations are small and scattered in many countries.

Movements: Hen Harriers migrate on a broad front, mainly to southern Europe, though a few cross to North Africa.

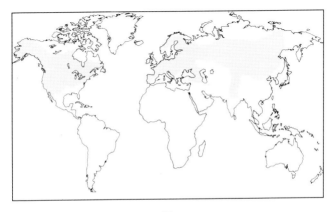

Pallid Harrier

Circus macrourus

Length:	43-48cm	**Eggs:**	3-6, bluish white
Wing:	333-381mm	**Incubation:**	28-30 days
Weight ♂:	295-325g	**Fledging:**	35-45 days
Weight ♀:	425-454g		

Identification: The male differs from the Hen Harrier in having generally paler coloration, especially on the head, and a less conspicuous white rump patch. Females and young birds are difficult to distinguish from Hen and Montagu's harriers, but can be identified by the clear pale collar. Compared with Montagu's, the black streak behind the eye is stronger.

Habitat: Open steppe grasslands, sometimes cornfields.

Nest: A ground nester like all harriers, the Pallid usually chooses an area of tall weeds or bushes for nesting. Less often, the nest is sited in open grassland or a marshy area. It varies from little more than a scrape to a pile of grass and weeds half a metre thick.

Food: Lemmings and other small rodents are the principal food source, and the harrier's breeding success is strongly affected by fluctuations in the numbers of these animals. When rodents are scarce, the Pallid Harrier takes birds such as larks, pipits and their young, as well as lizards, frogs and grasshoppers.

Range: From Eastern Europe and across Central Asia.

Movements: Migratory, wintering in Africa south of the Sahara, and in India. After good breeding years, wanderers occur in Western Europe, including Britain, Scandinavia and Germany.

Montagu's Harrier

Circus pygargus

Length:	41-46cm	**Eggs:**	4-5, bluish white
Wing:	332-383mm	**Incubation:**	27-30 days
Weight ♂:	227-305g	**Fledging:**	35-40 days
Weight ♀:	319-445g		

Identification: Males are distinguished from those of the Hen Harrier by a dark bar along the upperside of the wing, and reddish-brown streaks on the belly. Females and young birds are difficult to distinguish, but have an appreciably narrower white rump patch.

Habitat: Rough fields and grasslands, marshy areas, moorland and cereal fields.

Nest: Though often nesting solitarily, Montagu's Harrier will breed in small, loose colonies where numerous. As with the Hen Harrier, some males are bigamous. The nest is a flat pad of reeds and grasses, placed on the ground, but usually screened by tall vegetation.

Food: Rodents, especially Field Voles, form much of the prey, though larger species such as young rabbits are also taken. Small birds, lizards and frogs are consumed, as well as a good quantity of insects.

Range: From Britain right across Europe and Central Asia, with a small population in North Africa. This species expanded its range northwards early in the twentieth century, but has faced setbacks since, ranging from shooting and pesticide poisoning to nest destruction by mowing machines. It is still declining in most western European countries except Sweden and Denmark.

Movements: European breeders winter in Africa south of the Sahara, while more eastern populations move to India and Sri Lanka.

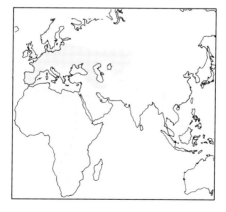

Dark Chanting Goshawk

Melierax metabates

Length:	38-48cm	**Eggs:**	1-2, bluish white
Wing:	305-333mm	**Incubation:**	not recorded
Weight ♂:	645-695g	**Fledging:**	not recorded
Weight ♀:	841-852g		

Identification: Although the adult plumage slightly resembles that of a male Hen Harrier, there should be little danger of confusion. This is a much shorter-winged bird which hunts at high speed, quite unlike the drifting flight of a foraging harrier. Its strongly barred tail is also characteristic. The brown-plumaged young could be confused with other hawks and buzzards, but the dark underparts with barred thighs and belly combined with a pale rump patch are distinctive.

Habitat: Typically a bird of tropical savannas or bush, sometimes venturing into plantations or semi-desert.

Nest: Sited from 5 to 10 metres up in a dense thorny tree, the nest is a small twig platform, sometimes cemented with mud, and lined with scraps such as skin, dung, rags and grass.

Food: Most food is taken on the ground; lizards, snakes and insects accounting for a large proportion. The bird also takes some mammals and birds, and is recorded killing prey as large as a guineafowl. Much of its prey is captured by surprise attacks as it dashes at high speed between trees, but it may also walk or run on the ground when foraging.

Range: Morocco, West and Central Africa and southwest Arabia.

Movements: Generally sedentary, but young birds may wander, and the species has once been recorded in Spain.

Goshawk

Accipiter gentilis

Length:	48-66cm	**Eggs:**	3 (1-5), unmarked pale blue
Wing:	318-381mm		or dirty white
Weight ♂:	600-1110g	**ncubation:**	36-38 days
Weight ♀:	820-2054g	**Fledging:**	80-90 days

Identification: The adult male has the back and wings blue-grey, shading into blackish on the crown. The white underside is finely barred with grey, and the white-tipped tail is crossed by a number of white-edged, broad, wavy bands. The female is similar, but brownish above.

Habitat: Generally, this is a bird of dense woodland, with a distinct preference for conifers.

Nest: The nest, which may be an old one refurbished or a new structure, is a large, untidy collection of dry sticks and twigs, either broken off by the bird's weight or bitten off with the bill. Sometimes there is a lining of green conifer sprigs and pieces of bark. The bird usually sites the nest between 10 and 20 metres above ground level in a large tree.

Food: The species feeds on birds and mammals up to the size of Black Grouse (to which it is particularly partial) and young hares. Occasionally nestling songbirds are taken, the bird returning time and again until the nest is empty.

Range: Distributed around the Northern Hemisphere, Goshawks breed in all European countries except Iceland, but numbers are small in most areas as the species has suffered greatly from persecution and environmental pollution. The population in Britain is gradually increasing, and has undoubtedly benefited from afforestation in some areas.

Movements: The species is a partial migrant, northern breeders being much more prone to move than southern ones, and most movement involving young birds. Most stay within Europe, though small numbers are seen crossing the Straits of Gibraltar and the Bosphorus.

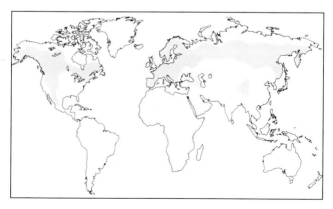

Sparrowhawk
Accipiter nisus

Length:	28-38cm	**Eggs:**	2-7, bluish white, blotched reddish brown
Wing:	178-254mm		
Weight ♂:	110-196g	**Incubation:**	33-35 days
Weight ♀:	185-342g	**Fledging:**	24-30 days

Identification: A small, short-winged hawk with a proportionately long tail. The much larger Goshawk has a distinctly longer, more forward-projecting head. Females are considerably larger than males, and browner plumaged.

Habitat: A woodland breeder, with a liking for conifer plantations, especially of larch. Smallish woods with more open country nearby are preferred to extensive tracts of unbroken forest, and females especially hunt a good deal in farmland and other open country after the breeding season.

Nest: A platform of sticks and twigs, those of larch being favoured where available. As incubation proceeds, the nest becomes flecked with pieces of white down from the female's body. Nests in conifers are usually placed across a group of lateral branches where they join the trunk. Unlike many larger raptors, a new nest is normally made each season. Nest height varies greatly, from about 2 metres to over 20.

Food: Sparrowhawks make good use of cover when hunting, flying fast and low through trees or along hedgerows, aiming to take small birds by surprise. They are extremely bold in pursuit of prey, sometimes dashing recklessly into thick bushes or human dwellings. Birds make up a good 98 per cent of its food in most places, though rodents may be taken when they are exceptionally abundant. As might be expected, females take larger prey on average, and are capable of killing birds up to the size of a Wood Pigeon.

Range: From Europe, North Africa and the Middle East, right across the centre of Asia as far as China and eastern Siberia.

Movements: Northern populations are migratory, more southerly ones only partially so or not at all. Like the larger soaring raptors, they make sea crossings at narrow straits, where spectacular numbers may sometimes be seen.

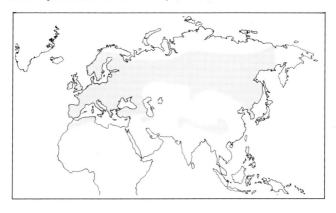

Levant Sparrowhawk

Accipiter brevipes

Length: 33-38cm
Wing: 216-241mm
Weight ♂: 150-223g
Weight ♀: 232-275g

Eggs: 3-5, pale bluish with small grey and brown markings
Incubation: 30-35 days
Fledging: 40-45 days

Identification: Slimmer than the Sparrowhawk, with more pointed wings which have conspicuously dark tips. The tail bars are less conspicuous, and males are generally much paler. A good view of a perched male shows it to have grey cheeks, unlike the rufous cheeks of a male Sparrowhawk.

Habitat: Deciduous woodland, with a preference for hilly country, and frequently nesting along river valleys.

Nest: Sited 5 to 10 metres up in a broad-leaved tree, the nest is a small stick structure lined with green leaves. The nest site is often situated near water.

Food: Small birds, but also a fair proportion of mammals including mice, squirrels and also bats. Reptiles, including snakes, are taken, and immature birds particularly eat many large insects. When hunting birds, its tactics are essentially the same as the Sparrowhawk's, but it finds most of its ground prey while watching from a perch.

Range: The Balkans, southern Russia and the Middle East. Counts at migration stations suggest that its population is a small one of about 2000 pairs.

Movements: Migratory, wintering in Africa, probably on the Ethiopian highlands. Large numbers pass through the Bosphorus and also Israel, while a smaller number use a more easterly route through the Caucasus.

Shikra

Accipiter badius

		Eggs:	2-7, pale greenish or
Length:	31-36cm		bluish, usually unmarked
Wing:	165-267mm	**Incubation:**	30-35 days
Weight ♂:	136-193g	**Fledging:**	not recorded
Weight ♀:	266g		

T. BOYER

Identification: Smaller than Levant Sparrowhawk, with more rounded wings, but otherwise resembling it in colour pattern. A good view of a perched bird would show five or six tail bars whilst the Levant Sparrowhawk has six to eight.

Habitat: A savanna species, but also found around cultivation and villages, and in churchyards and wooded river banks.

Nest: A flimsy stick platform, lined with a few green leaves. It is placed from 5 to 15 metres up, generally well out on a side branch.

Food: Small birds, small mammals, including bats, and large insects. Most prey are taken from the ground, but some on the wing. It will snatch lizards from walls, and plunders nestlings from sparrows' nests.

Range: From the southern USSR to China, and throughout Africa south of the Sahara. It is only a sporadic breeder in the Western Palearctic area covered by this book.

Movements: Northern breeding birds are migratory, wintering from Iran to northwestern India. There is evidence that the migrants are mainly young birds.

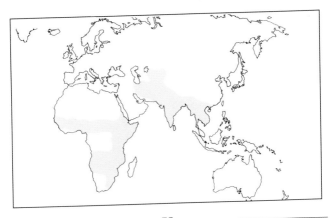

Common Buzzard

Buteo buteo

Length:	51-56cm	**Eggs:**	2-6, white with reddish-brown markings
Wing:	343-419mm		
Weight ♂:	427-1183g	**Incubation:**	33-35 days
Weight ♀:	486-1364g	**Fledging:**	40-50 days

Identification: Although often mistaken for an eagle, the Buzzard's flight silhouette is quite different, even when its smaller size is not apparent. Its wings are proportionately shorter, and the head appears shorter and more rounded. More of a problem in much of northern Europe is confusion with the Honey Buzzard. The Common Buzzard's plumage is extremely variable, but its flight outline is distinguished by a broader head and relatively longer, more rounded tail. When

soaring, the Common Buzzard holds the wings slightly raised but the Honey Buzzard keeps them flat.

Habitat: Mixed terrain with small woods and spinneys studded about in open country is typical habitat. Where larger tracts of forest are found, Buzzards will only be found on the edges. The surrounding open land can vary from meadows and marshland to moorland and mountainous areas.

Nest: A large pile of sticks or heather, lined with green sprays or sometimes seaweed or rushes. It is placed either in the fork of a tree or bush, not necessarily very high, or on a cliff ledge. Several nests are maintained by a pair, and used roughly in rotation from one year to the next.

Food: A wide variety of ground-living prey is taken, particularly small mammals. In Britain, rabbits have for long been a major prey, and consequently Buzzards were severely affected during the era when rabbits were almost wiped out by myxomatosis. Some birds are included, mainly young, and also reptiles, amphibians, and some insects and earthworms. Carrion is also eaten, particularly during winter months.

Range: Throughout Europe and Central Asia to Siberia and Japan. A good deal of geographical variation occurs over this wide range.

Movements: British and many Western European Buzzards are sedentary, but northern and eastern populations migrate. Huge numbers pass over Gibraltar, the Bosphorus and the Caucasus. In the latter area as many as 135,000 have been counted in a single day.

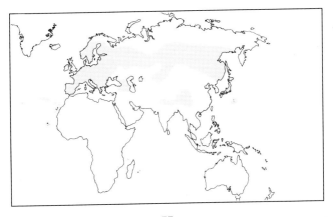

Rough-legged Buzzard
Buteo lagopus

Length:	51-61cm	**Eggs:**	3-4 (6), white, with brown markings
Wing:	393-482mm		
Weight ♂:	600-930g	**Incubation:**	28-31 days
Weight ♀:	948-1280g	**Fledging:**	41 days

Identification: The head is whitish brown, with the back somewhat darker brown, and the tail is white, with many black bars, the subterminal one being rather broader. Below, it is dusky-white with dark brown mottling, and usually with a dark belly band. The feathered tarsi, from which the species derives its name, are barred whitish and brown.

Habitat: The Rough-legged Buzzard is a bird of open country and mountainsides, and frequents timber country only if it contains many open areas.

Nest: Normally sited on a rock ledge under an overhang, but occasionally in a tree, the nest is a small structure of twigs of dwarf willow or other Arctic plants, with a deep greenery-lined cup. The pair has several alternative nests which are used in annual rotation.

Food: Small mammals up to the size of rabbits form the bulk of the species' diet, with lemmings being particularly favoured in the Arctic. When mammals are in short supply, the Rough-legged Buzzard preys more on birds.

Range: The species breeds across northern Scandinavia and the USSR.

Movements: Fully migratory, the Rough-legged Buzzard's movements are strongly influenced by the fluctuations of rodent numbers in the breeding areas. When rodent numbers are high, movement may not begin until October, but in poor years, birds may leave in August. Wintering areas may be as far south as Spain and North Africa, and young birds returning north to breed for the first time may settle in areas 1000 km or more from their birthplace.

Long-legged Buzzard
Buteo rufinus

Length: 51-66cm
Wing: 419-495mm
Weight ♂: 590-1281g
Weight ♀: 945-1760g

Eggs: 3-4, white with reddish-brown blotches
Incubation: 28-31 days
Fledging: c.41 days

Identification: Slightly larger than the Common Buzzard, but with a very similar flight outline. Identification features of adults are the pale unbarred tail and dark belly contrasting with pale breast and head. Young birds have pale bars on the tail, and can be very difficult to distinguish from Common Buzzards.

Habitat: Typically arid steppes and semi-desert areas, but also wooded hills and mountainous areas.

Nest: Commonly sited on a cliff ledge, or in a tree where available. A bulky stick structure, it is lined with finer material such as woodland straw.

Food: Mainly small mammals, such as gerbils and lemmings, but varying considerably according to the prey locally available. Some reptiles, including venomous snakes are taken, and a few birds up to the size of a pheasant. Like the Common Buzzard it will feed on carrion in winter. Food is located both by soaring and from a perch, and it occasionally forages on the ground for prey.

Range: The Balkans, North Africa and the Middle East. There is some evidence to suggest that the species has been gradually increasing its range in a northwesterly direction. The Balkan population is probably less than 100 pairs.

Movements: Northern populations are migratory, southern ones only partially so. No great numbers are recorded from the main migration stations.

Upland Buzzard
Buteo hemilasius

Length:	c.71cm	**Eggs:**	2-4, buffy white, blotched red-brown
Wing:	445-504mm		
Weight ♂:	950-1400g	**Incubation:**	c.30 days
Weight ♀:	970-2050g	**Fledging:**	c.45 days

Identification: A very large buzzard, with pale head, pale barred tail (appearing almost white in flight), rusty under wing coverts, and a broad dark rear edge to the wing.

Habitat: Steppe, plains, mountains and deserts.

Nest: Built on low cliffs or even steep river banks, the nest is rather small for the size of the bird, generally less than a metre across. It is made of sticks, and lined with grass, hair or wool. Like other buzzards, a pair generally maintains more than one nest, using them in rotation.

Food: Mainly small mammals; pikas (distinctive Central Asian relatives of rabbits) appear to be favoured where they occur. Ground birds such as larks and pipits, and some large species such as sandgrouse, ptarmigan and snowcock are also recorded as taken by this species.

Range: Central Asia, south to Tibet.

Movements: Migrates in winter to northern India, Burma, China and Korea. An immature bird has wandered to Romania.

Lesser Spotted Eagle
Aquila pomarina

Length:	61-66cm	**Eggs:**	1-3, white with red-brown
Wing:	445-508mm		and grey markings
Weight:	1325-	**Incubation:**	43 days
	1975g	**Fledging:**	50-55 days

Identification: Although only the size of a buzzard, this species still shows a typical eagle flight profile with long projecting head, long broad wings and short tail. The chief problem is to distinguish it from the Greater Spotted Eagle. Adults seen from below are easily identified; the wing linings of the Lesser Spotted are paler than the flight feathers, but in the Greater Spotted, the linings are the darker of the two. This difference is less marked in immature birds, whose pale

spotted upperparts (in both species) give rise to the English name. However, the pale spots are larger in the Lesser Spotted Eagle, which also has a pale nape patch, absent in the larger species.

Habitat: Clearings in damp forests, or forest edge adjoining swampy areas, are typical breeding habitat. Hunting birds concentrate on marshy areas, but also patrol grassland. Savanna is the winter terrain.

Nest: Built in a tree fork, the nest averages about 15 metres up, yet is not usually placed at the very top of the tree. It is made of sticks, and replenished with green branches. First nests are quite small, but with repeated use they can become about a metre across and 70cm deep.

Food: Mainly mammals, ranging from voles to rabbits, supplemented with a wide variety of other prey. This includes ground birds and their young, lizards and frogs, and large insects, especially beetles and grasshoppers. Prey are located either from a perch, or while circling at low altitude, and also quite regularly while walking about on the ground.

Range: A patchy distribution, with populations in Central and Eastern Europe, the Caucasus, and India and northern Burma.

Movements: Lesser Spotted Eagles winter in East African savannas from the Sudan to Mozambique and Namibia. Concentrating at narrow straits like other soaring raptors, the Lesser Spotted Eagle is seen in greatest numbers at the Bosphorus, where as many as 19,000 have been counted during an autumn.

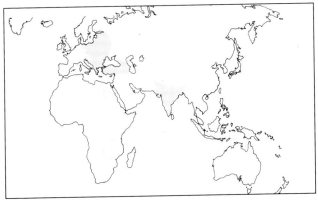

Greater Spotted Eagle
Aquila clanga

Length:	66-74cm	**Eggs:**	1-3, greyish white, unmarked or with a few greyish brown spots
Wing:	495-546mm		
Weight ♂:	1665-1925g	**Incubation:**	42-44 days
Weight ♀:	1770-2520g	**Fledging:**	60-65 days

Identification: Larger on average than the Lesser Spotted Eagle, but there is some overlap; the main differences are discussed under that species. Compared with the Tawny Eagle, the Spotted Eagles are both slimmer with proportionately broader wings and squarer tails.

Habitat: Large forests, with lakes or swampy areas, but also some smaller stands of trees provided they are near water. In steppe areas, the bird is only found along river valleys.

Nest: Built in trees, usually large ones, but in steppe country sometimes in low bushes, or even on the ground. The usual height of European nests is 8 to12 metres. When first built, the stick nest is quite small for the size of the bird, but used year after year it gradually becomes very large. Green sprays are brought in at intervals while nesting, and some grass is used in the lining.

Food: Very varied, with small mammals predominating if they are sufficiently abundant, but with birds, amphibians and reptiles substituted if they are not. Its liking for wet areas shows in the inclusion of such species as coots and ducks, water voles, frogs and occasional fish. Greater Spotted Eagles sometimes specialize in raiding bird colonies for unfledged young; herons, Black-headed Gulls and Rooks are among its victims. Like its smaller relative, it obtains a good deal of food while walking on the ground; both species have relatively long legs, with reduced feathering compared with other *Aquila* eagles. Carrion is occasionally taken.

Range: Finland and Eastern Europe, through Siberia to Amurland.

Movements: Migratory, wintering in southern Europe, North Africa, the Middle East and northern India. In contrast to the Lesser Spotted Eagle, it migrates on a broad front, and does not appear in large numbers at the usual migration stations.

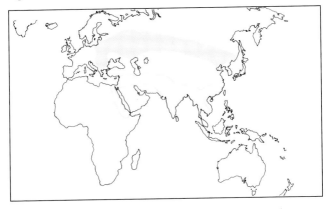

Tawny Eagle
Aquila rapax

Length:	66-79cm	**Eggs:**	1-3, white, unmarked, or faintly marked with brown
Wing:	482-559mm	**Incubation:**	c.45 days
Weight:	1572-2378g	**Fledging:**	55-70 days

Identification: This numerous and widespread species is also highly variable, and its two northern races are often separated as a distinct species called the Steppe Eagle, *Aquila nipalensis*. They are generally uniform dark brown in colour. The North African and southern Asian forms are the most variable, individuals ranging from uniform dark to pale yellowish, but nearly always showing a pale area on the primaries in flight. Differences from the Greater Spotted Eagle have been mentioned under that species. Dark individuals could also be confused with the Imperial Eagle, but are relatively broader-winged and shorter-tailed, and seen from below show a contrast between the dark body and pale wing linings.

Habitat: Open country of all types, from cultivated areas to deserts and grassland to savannas. Only forests are avoided.

Nest: Nest sites may be on trees from 3 to 30 metres up, on small hillocks or haystacks, or on cliffs. The nest is quite small for that of an eagle, perhaps because it is less often reused in later years than those of most species. The sticks used to construct it are often thorny, and it is lined with grass or straw. This is a highly gregarious species, and when food supplies permit, nests may be as little as 300 metres apart.

Food: European and Central Asian birds specialize in taking sousliks (ground squirrels), supplemented by other small rodents, ground birds (including young Great Bustards), snakes, lizards and insects. Southern breeders, and all races in their winter quarters, take a wider range of food, including a fair amount of carrion. Wintering birds move about in flocks, and will gather at carcasses with vultures. They also congregate at food sources such as locust and termite swarms.

Range: The two northern races sometimes treated as the Steppe Eagle breed from Eastern Europe across Central Asia to Mongolia. The more variable southern two races breed from Morocco, across North Africa, and from Afghanistan to Bengal and Burma.

Movements: The southern races are not migratory, but the two northern races undertake long journeys. European birds winter within the range of the North African population, as well as further south in East Africa, and in the Middle East. Central Asian birds winter in India.

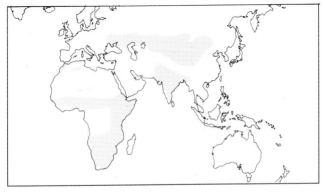

Imperial Eagle
Aquila heliaca

Length:	78-84cm	**Eggs:**	2-3, buffish white with a few grey, brown or purplish markings
Wing:	571-660mm		
Weight ♂:	2450-2718g	**Incubation:**	43 days
Weight ♀:	3160-4530g	**Fledging:**	65-77 days

Identification: A large and impressive species, averaging only a little smaller than the Golden Eagle. The long, broad wings have more nearly parallel front and rear edges than the

Golden, and the tail is more distinctly two-coloured. Adults of the Spanish race are easily recognized by their white shoulders, but these are much smaller in eastern birds, and entirely lacking in immatures of both races.

Habitat: Very variable, ranging from forested mountains to plains with only scattered trees.

Nest: A huge stick structure in a tree, often over 2 metres across and deep. Grass, finer twigs and green leaves are used in the lining. A pair usually maintains two or three nests, and uses them in rotation.

Food: Rabbits are important prey for the Spanish birds; sousliks and hares for the eastern race. A good many birds are taken by both forms, including such large species as bustards, ducks, geese and flamingos. A smaller proportion of the diet is provided by reptiles, including some venomous snakes, and insects. Carrion is also taken, mainly in winter.

Range: Spain and southeast Europe and across Central Asia as far as Tibet and northwest India. The European populations have been seriously reduced, mainly by persecution; at present, the Spanish race (which formerly also occurred in Portugal) consists of only 30 to 40 pairs. In Eastern Europe, Romania is the stronghold, with about 100 pairs.

Movements: The Spanish population is non-migratory, but Eastern European birds migrate to North Africa and the Middle East in winter, mostly passing across the Bosphorus. Birds from further east, in Asia, winter from East Africa across to India.

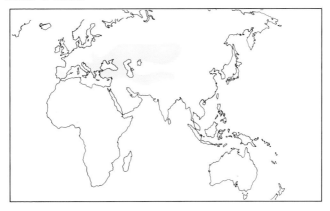

Golden Eagle
Aquila chrysaetos

Length:	76-89cm	**Eggs:**	2, dull white, blotched
Wing:	571-711mm		red-brown and grey
Weight ♂:	2840-4550g	**Incubation:**	45 days
Weight ♀:	3840-6665g	**Fledging:**	80 days

Identification: The entire upperside is dark brown (paler in some individuals), with the lanceolate crown and nape feathers edged with gold. The tail has a number of irregular dark grey bands. Below, the bird is somewhat paler brown than above, with the thigh feathering shaded buff, and the legs and feet yellow.

Habitat: This is largely a bird of the most inhospitable and extensive open mountainous areas of the Northern Hemisphere, though in areas where the human population is small they are also found in low-lying country.

Nest: The untidy nest of sticks and branches is most often sited on a rocky crag (although occasionally in a tree), and over the course of many seasons it can become enormous. Most pairs have a number of alternative sites, which are used in rotation.

Food: The Golden Eagle preys on a wide variety of mammals up to the size of a small deer fawn, and some gamebirds, all invariably taken on the ground. It undoubtedly does eat domestic lambs, and even sheep on occasion, but in such cases the prey is probably already dead, or at least extremely sick.

Range: Scandinavia and Eastern Europe form the most extensive breeding area, but Golden Eagles occur in mountainous places in several other parts of Europe and the Middle East. Scotland remains the British stronghold.

Movements: The Golden Eagle is a partial migrant, with duals from the coldest northerly part of the range moving south for the winter.

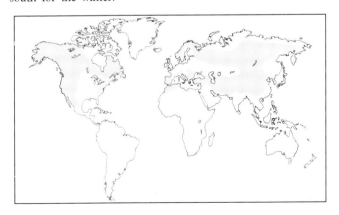

Verreaux's Eagle

Aquila verreauxii

Length:	79-97cm	**Eggs:**	2, bluish white, sometimes sparsely marked red-brown
Wing:	559-635mm		
Weight ♂:	3600g	**Incubation:**	43-46 days
Weight ♀:	3680-5779g	**Fledging:**	95-99 days

Identification: Given even a moderately good view, the adult is unmistakable - a large, black eagle with white lower back and rump, and striking white patches on the primaries. Young birds are dull brown, but still have the pale wing patches, and a narrow white rump. Even in silhouette, a flying Verreaux's Eagle is easy to identify by the characteristic wing shape, with the rear edge curved outwards, narrowing again at the base. Exceptional powers of flight surpass even those of the Golden Eagle.

Habitat: Remote, rocky mountainous country.

Nest: A flattish mass of sticks, over 2 metres across, sited on a cliff ledge. Fresh green branches are added to the nest throughout the breeding cycle.

Food: Largely mammals, especially Rock Hyraxes. Small antelopes and hares are also captured by this bold and powerful species. Bird prey includes francolins and guineafowl. Lizards are occasionally recorded.

Range: Eastern and southern Africa, but a few apparently breed in Sinai, and there have been breeding attempts in Israel.

Movements: Not migratory, though young birds may wander extensively.

Bonelli's Eagle
Hieraaetus fasciatus

Length:	66-74cm	**Eggs:**	2, white, sparsely marked
Wing:	406-559mm		with brown and lilac
Weight:	1712-	**Incubation:**	37-40 days
	2386g	**Fledging:**	c.65 days

Identification: Longer tail and eagle-like wings with more 'fingered' primary tips give Bonelli's Eagle a different silhouette from the Honey Buzzard, the bird with which it is most easily confused. If plumage features can be seen, adult birds are unmistakable due to the contrast between a white body and dark wings as seen from below. Banking to show its upperside, another characteristic feature is the pale area in the middle of the back. Young birds are also distinctive, with pale rufous underwing coverts, demarcated by a narrow dark band along the rear edge, and pale flight feathers contrasting with dark primary tips. The African race is blacker above and even paler below, and sometimes regarded as a distinct

species called the African Hawk-eagle, *Hieraaetus spilogaster*.

Habitat: In Europe and Asia Bonelli's Eagle occurs chiefly in mountainous areas with woods or scrub vegetation. The African race occurs in savanna, forest edge and cultivated areas, not necessarily mountainous.

Nest: European and Asian birds normally nest on cliff ledges, sometimes on a building, or in a tree, while the African race usually builds in a tree, 10 to 40 metres up. The nest is often as much as 2 metres across, though sometimes smaller where space is limited. It is made of quite large sticks considering this is only a medium-sized eagle. A pair may maintain up to five nests, choosing one at the start of the breeding season and refurbishing it with green sprays.

Food: A powerful and aggressive predator for its size, taking a wide variety of prey, often quite large. Hares and rabbits, and hyraxes in Africa, are frequent mammal victims, while birds include pigeons, herons, ducks, guineafowl and gulls. Other raptors are sometimes taken as well. Lizards form only a small proportion of the diet. Its usual hunting tactic is a swift dash from the cover of a tree, though some prey is spotted while patrolling mountain slopes. Though most prey are seized from the ground, Bonelli's Eagle is fully capable of catching birds in flight.

Range: The warmer regions of Europe and Asia, south Burma and Africa south of the Sahara. European populations have been much reduced by persecution.

Movements: Non-migratory, although young birds may wander.

Booted Eagle

Hieraaetus pennatus

Length:	46-53cm	**Eggs:**	2, white with brown markings
Wing:	355-431mm		
Weight ♂:	510-770g	**Incubation:**	36-38 days
Weight ♀:	840-1250g	**Fledging:**	50-60 days

Identification: A small eagle which could be confused with one of the buzzards but for its proportionately longer, narrower wings and tail. It occurs in two distinct colour phases. The dark phase is chocolate-coloured, with a paler tail, and could be confused with a Marsh Harrier but for its completely different habits and flight. The pale phase is highly distinctive when seen overhead, with a white body and wing linings contrasting with blackish flight feathers. Both colour phases seen from above show a contrast between pale wing coverts and dark flight feathers.

Habitat: Wooded hills and mountains, with scattered areas of open country. Oak woods are particularly favoured for breeding.

Nest: Normally placed in a tree, 6 to 16 metres up, the nest is somewhat more than a metre across and made of sticks with a lining of pine shoots or green leaves. Cliffs are occasionally used in Morocco.

Food: A versatile and dashing hunter, which takes a good many birds. Prey is seized from the ground or among foliage after a high-speed stoop. Mammal prey includes sousliks, young rabbits, hamsters, rats and stoats, while birds range from small songbirds up to partridges. Colonial species such as herons may be raided for nestlings. Reptiles, especially lizards, are also taken.

Range: Southern Europe, North Africa and Central Asia. The European population has decreased mainly due to habitat loss.

Movements: Migratory, European birds wintering in Africa south of the Sahara, while Asian birds move to India.

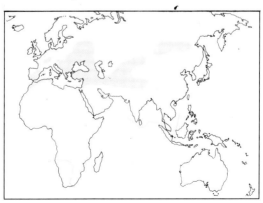

FALCONS

Family FALCONIDAE

Lesser Kestrel
Falco naumanni

Length:	30cm	**Eggs:**	3-6, buffish, speckled yellowish-red
Wing:	224-246mm	**Incubation:**	28 days
Weight:	90-172g	**Fledging:**	26-28 days

Identification: Smaller and slimmer than the Common Kestrel, with a more pointed tail. Adult males show an unspotted back and a wide blue-grey area on the wing. Females and young of the two species are much more similar, but can be distinguished at very close range by their pale claws. For all plumages, however, the gregarious and noisy life-style of this species is the best means of identification.

Habitat: Open dry country and rocky areas.

Nest: Like all falcons, the Lesser Kestrel makes no nest beyond a scrape. The usual site chosen by this species is a ledge on a cliff or building. Rarely, tree cavities may be used. This is a strongly colonial breeder, nesting in groups from a few to some 200 pairs.

Food: Very largely insects, especially grasshoppers and beetles. Most are taken from the ground, but some insects such as termites are captured in the air. Some small rodents are taken, especially in spring, but very few birds. The Lesser Kestrel hovers less often while hunting than does the Common Kestrel.

Range: The warmer regions of Europe and Central Asia, from the Mediterranean east to China.

Movements: Most winter in Africa south of the Sahara, ranging further south on the east side of the continent. Smaller numbers winter in India. It is the most numerous falcon in winter in South Africa. Migration is on a broad front, so the species is not especially numerous at the classic raptor migration stations.

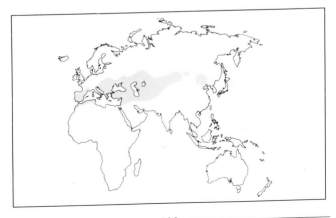

American Kestrel
Falco sparverius

Length:	27cm	**Eggs:**	4 (3-7), white to pale pink, heavily brown-marked	
Wing:	165-203mm	**Incubation:**	29-30 days	
Weight:	100-120g	**Fledging:**	30 days	

Identification: The slate-grey crown is partly bordered with black, and often has a central rufous patch. The rufous back is flecked with black, while the plain rufous tail has a black terminal band and a narrow white tip. The wings are blue-grey with scattered black markings, and the primaries are black. The cheeks, bordered by two vertical black bars, and the throat, are white; the rest of the underparts are varying

shades of rufous, becoming paler towards the tail, and with black spotting in the lower regions. The eye is brown, and the legs and feet are orange-yellow. The female is less colourful, with rufous replacing much of the grey, and more extensive black spotting on the back and tail, where the terminal band is much narrower.

Habitat: The only indigenous American Kestrel, this attractive little falcon is found in all types of open country, preferably where there are some trees, as well as in suburbs, and even city centres.

Nest: The species builds no nest, choosing instead to lay its eggs in any suitable cavity in a tree, rock-face or even a building. Occasionally, the birds will use the disused nest of some other species.

Food: The American Kestrel's main diet consists of large insects, particularly grasshoppers, but when these are not available it preys on mice and small birds, and occasionally on lizards, scorpions and amphibians. The bird has also been known to prey on swarms of small bats.

Range: The species ranges from the tree-line of Alaska and Canada, south through the entire United States into northern and western Mexico, and down to the extreme south of South America. It is an extremely rare vagrant to Western Europe.

Movements: Birds breeding north of about 40°N migrate south in autumn, along with some more southerly-breeding birds, to winter in southern Florida and many parts of Mexico.

Common Kestrel
Falco tinnunculus

Length: 33-36cm
Wing: 216-279mm
Weight ♂: 136-252g
Weight ♀: 154-314g

Eggs: 4 (2-6), whitish, heavily marked red-brown
Incubation: 28 days
Fledging: 28-30 days

Identification: The crown and nape are grey, with black shaft-streaks, while the rest of the upperparts are chestnut, marked with black pear-shaped spots of varying sizes. The primaries are deep black-brown. The face has a dark

moustachial stripe, and the underparts are buff, spotted with black-brown. The blue-grey tail has a broad black subterminal band and a narrow white tip, and the legs are yellow. The female lacks the grey on the head and tail, is more heavily spotted, and has many narrow black bars across the tail.

Habitat: This is a bird of open tree-scattered country from sea level up to at least 4500 metres, but it is absent from densely-forested areas, high mountain regions, and harsh deserts.

Nest: No nest is built. A cavity or hollow in a tree is a common breeding site, but similar situations among rocks, and in or on man-made structures such as buildings, bridges, pylons and even bale-ricks are equally acceptable, as are disused nests of other species such as crows (Corvidae). Due to this variety of sites, the nest may be at any level, from a metre or so above ground to over 30 metres.

Food: The species' main prey consists of small mammals, but it also take small to medium-sized birds, lizards, small snakes, frogs, and a variety of insects.

Range: A species found over much of the Old World, the Common Kestrel breeds throughout Europe except for Iceland and the far north.

Movements: Birds breeding in the far north are highly migratory, especially the eastern populations, from which some birds winter south of the Sahara. Southern breeders are sedentary, while in central regions, including Britain, movements are highly variable and to some extent influenced by food supply.

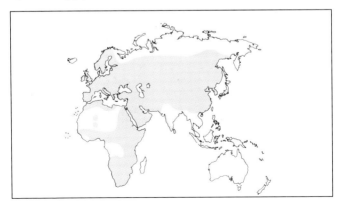

Red-footed Falcon
Falco vespertinus

Length:	30cm	**Eggs:**	2-5, buffish, with dense red-brown markings
Wing:	216-254mm	**Incubation:**	22-27 days
Weight:	130-197g	**Fledging:**	26-27 days

Identification: Adult males, with their striking dark grey plumage and contrasting red thighs, are easily recognized. However, the browner, barred females and immatures can easily be confused with the Common and Lesser kestrels, and like them hover frequently while hunting. The longer, more pointed wings of this species give it a different flight silhouette, somewhat resembling that of the Hobby, though longer tailed. Females have a characteristically pale head, contrasting with the darker upperparts. Young males go

through a complex series of plumage changes as they mature. In the eastern race, adult males have striking white wing linings; this form is sometimes regarded as a separate species called the Amur Falcon, *Falco amurensis*.

Habitat: For breeding, the Red-footed Falcon frequents grasslands with scattered woods, marsh and river valleys and forest clearings. Savanna is its winter habitat.

Nest: Old nests of other birds, especially members of the crow family, provide the usual nest sites. As this is usually a colonial breeder, it prefers the nests of the colonial crow, the Rook.

Food: Adults feed principally on insects, and catch much of their prey in the air. Grasshoppers, beetles, dragonflies, bees and many others are recorded in the breeding areas, and termites are important in the winter quarters. Larger prey are taken while rearing young, including small mammals and birds, lizards and frogs.

Range: Central and Eastern Europe and across Central Asia as far as Manchuria and China. Most winter in Africa south of the Sahara, as far as Cape Province and Namibia. There are indications of a trend towards a westward extension of the breeding range.

Movements: Red-footed Falcons are sociable on migration and in winter quarters, travelling in large flocks, and roosting in gatherings of up to 5000 birds. Migrants pass through the Middle East and eastern Mediterranean, but vagrants to Western Europe, including Britain, occur fairly regularly, especially in spring.

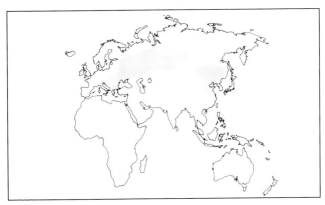

Merlin

Falco columbarius

Length:	27-33cm	**Eggs:**	6 (2-7), pale buff, heavily marked red-brown
Wing:	190-228mm		
Weight ♂:	125-234g	**Incubation:**	28-32 days
Weight ♀:	164-300g	**Fledging:**	25-30 days

Identification: The upperparts are slate-blue, darker on the crown, with fine black streaking throughout; there is also an indistinct dark moustachial stripe, and a broad rufous collar. The tail has a dark subterminal band, and a pale grey tip. Below, the plumage is pale rufous, marked with black-brown streaks and spots, and the legs are yellow. The female is browner than the male, but has more tail bands.

Habitat: The tiny, fast-flying Merlin is a bird of thinly-wooded or open country, including the sea-shore, marshlands, grasslands and deserts. It frequents forested regions only if they also provide open hunting areas.

Nest: Most often the nest is a ground-scrape, usually in dense low vegetation, but sometimes a bulky nest of grasses and other stems is formed, probably by the incubating bird plucking material from the immediate surroundings. In woodland, the birds usually take over the disused nests of crows (Corvidae), and may be anywhere between 1.5 and 20 metres above the ground.

Food: The Merlin is a bold hunter of birds, occasionally rather bigger than itself, but it also takes some small mammals, lizards, snakes and insects, especially dragonflies.

Range: Scandinavia, including Iceland, Britain and the northern USSR are its breeding range. Its numbers in all these areas have shown a steady decrease this century. Merlins also breed in the north of the New World.

Movements: Most Merlins migrate south in autumn to wintering areas from Britain and southern Scandinavia to North Africa and the Middle East.

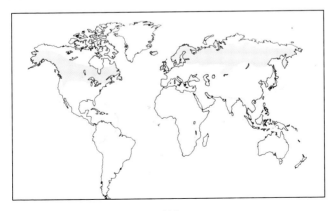

Hobby
Falco subbuteo

Length:	30-36cm	**Eggs:**	2-3, creamy-white, densely speckled red-brown
Wing:	241-279mm		
Weight ♂:	131-232g	**Incubation:**	28 days
Weight ♀:	141-340g	**Fledging:**	28-32 days

Identification: The upperparts are brownish grey, somewhat lighter on the tail, and becoming darker on the crown; the nape has a whitish half-collar, and the cream-coloured cheeks are marked with conspicuous long black moustaches. The underparts are buff, with the breast and belly heavily streaked with black and, when visible, the thighs and undertail are strikingly rufous. The legs and feet are yellow.

Habitat: In the breeding season, this fast and graceful flier is a bird of lower-altitude open country with scattered belts of woodland, avoiding damp locations. At other times of the year it seems to prefer savanna, grassland, sparse woodland and even areas of cultivation.

Nest: The birds select the disused nest of a large raptor or crow in which to lay their eggs; very occasionally, an old squirrel's drey may be used.

Food: The bird's extremely rapid flight enables it to easily capture all types of aerial prey, including birds up to thrush size and insects as large as locusts. Bats and small terrestrial mammals are also sometimes taken.

Range: The species occurs throughout Europe, in all suitable habitats, as far north as about 65°N.

Movements: In autumn, Hobbies migrate south in huge flocks to overwinter in tropical Africa, although there are a few winter records from Europe.

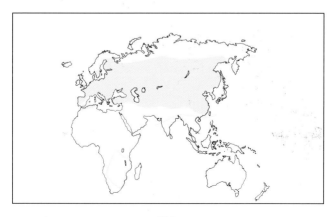

Eleonora's Falcon
Falco eleonorae

Length:	36-40cm	**Eggs:**	2-3, pink-white, blotched brown
Wing:	312-347mm	**Incubation:**	28 days
Weight:	340-450g	**Fledging:**	28-35 days

T. BOYER.

Identification: The species is uniformly dark sooty-brown above, with the tail a paler sooty-grey. The chin, throat and ear-coverts are whitish buff, and there is a broad, black-brown moustachial streak; the rest of the underside is rufous, washed or streaked with black, and the legs and feet are pale yellow.

Habitat: The bird is apparently restricted to rocky coastlines, islets and coastal tablelands.

Nest: The species breeds colonially on coastal cliff-ledges or small caves, usually no more than 10 metres from the sea, and no nest-material is used.

Food: Eleonora's Falcon is a superb aerial feeder, capturing small birds and insects in flight; very occasionally, it takes bats, small mammals and lizards. The bird's breeding season coincides with the southward migration of European passerines as they cross the Mediterranean; they take far more than their immediate needs, neatly storing the surplus for the future.

Range: The species is restricted to well-established colonies, many of which are inaccessible, along the Mediterranean coastal cliffs and on off-shore islands.

Movements: At the end of its breeding season, which is in autumn, the species migrates southeast along the Red Sea and East African coast, to overwinter in Madagascar.

Sooty Falcon

Falco concolor

Length: 33-36cm   **Eggs:**   1-4, pale buff, spotted brown
Wing: 254-292mm   **Incubation:** not recorded
Weight: not recorded   **Fledging:**   not recorded

Identification: Easily confused with a dark phase Eleonora's
Falcon, except at close range when the distinctly paler grey
plumage becomes apparent. Slightly smaller than Eleonora's,
it also has a more pointed tail, and tends to fly with the
wings more angled backwards.

Habitat: Arid and rocky areas, including deserts. Some breeding sites are on rocky islands.

Nest: Caves or crevices on cliffs or crags, sometimes underneath bushes. Sooty Falcons breed in rather loose colonies of up to 100 pairs.

Food: A bird specialist like Eleonora's Falcon, which similarly breeds during autumn in order to take advantage of the plentiful supply of migrant passerines when feeding its young. Prey taken range from warbler size up to hoopoes and orioles. In winter quarters it changes to a largely insect diet, taking locusts, termites and dragonflies, varied with a few bats.

Range: The complete breeding range of this somewhat mysterious species is still uncertain. Known breeding places are in the deserts of Libya, Egypt and Arabia, sometimes in Israel, and on islands in the Red Sea.

Movements: The main wintering area is Madagascar, but some birds also occur in coastal regions of East Africa, and on Indian Ocean islands.

Lanner Falcon
Falco biarmicus

Length: 34-50cm
Wing: 305-381mm

Weight ♂: 500-600g
Weight ♀: 700-900g

Eggs: 3 (3-4) pale creamy-white, heavily speckled purplish-brown
Incubation: c.30 days
Fledging: c.40 days

Identification: The crown and nape are rufous, edged with a fine black line, and there is a fine but distinct black moustachial stripe on the white cheeks. The rest of the upperparts are steely brown, and the whitish-tipped tail is pale greyish-brown, crossed by ten to twelve darker bands. The white underparts are heavily spotted brown-grey, and the feet are yellow.

Habitat: This is a bird of open arid country with sparse vegetation, and is even found on mountain slopes, below the snow-line.

Nest: The birds will nest either on a crag, selecting a pile of rocks, or in the nest of a buzzard, raven or similar species, or they will use the stick-nest of such species, sited in a tree. They are not averse to ousting the rightful occupants of such nests.

Food: Small to medium-sized birds form the bulk of the species' diet, but terrestrial mammals and lizards are also taken, as are large insects. Much prey is killed on the ground, although the Lanner is fully capable of dealing with its victims in the air.

Range: The species is found mainly in southwestern Europe, particularly on the Italian mainland in very small numbers, but it may prove to be more widespread across southern Europe than present data suggests.

Movements: Little is known about the species' movements, but it is known to descend to lower altitudes for the winter. Our present knowledge indicates little, if any, long-distance migration; however, further studies are required.

Saker Falcon
Falco cherrug

Length:	45-55cm	**Eggs:**	3-6, creamy-brown, heavily spotted reddish to nearly black
Wing:	333-419mm		
Weight ♂:	730-950g	**Incubation:**	28 days
Weight ♀:	970-1300g	**Fledging:**	40-45 days

T. BOYER

Identification: The black-streaked crown and nape are whitish buff, and the back and wings are sepia, with the rufous feather-edges producing an overall reddish cast. The tail is pale brown, with large, oval white spots on the outer feathers. The entire underparts are white, with dark brown spotting, becoming heavier and denser towards the tail. The eye is dark brown; the legs and feet yellow.

Habitat: The species is a bird of wooded steppes and foothills, with adjacent open country for hunting, up to about 4000 metres.

Nest: The birds usually select the disused nest of some other species, such as eagles, buzzards and vultures (Accipitridae), as high as 20 metres up in a large tree. Alternatively, the birds may select a bare, rocky ledge. Some pairs have two or three sites, which are used in rotation.

Food: The bulk of the species' prey consists of small mammals, but small lizards, small to medium-sized birds, and even large insects, are also taken.

Range: The species occurs mainly in the USSR, but has been recorded, apparently as an accidental vagrant, from parts of Europe, including Germany and Poland, and as far northwest as Sweden.

Movements: The species is migratory in some areas, and only partially so in others, the autumnal movements being in a southerly to southwesterly direction.

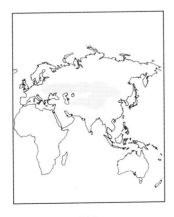

Gyr Falcon

Falco rusticolus

Length:	51-61cm	**Eggs:**	4 (2-7), white to buff,
Wing:	343-419mm		usually spotted red
Weight ♂:	805-1300g	**Incubation:**	28-29 days
Weight ♀:	1400-2100g	**Fledging:**	46-49 days

Identification: The Gyr Falcon is extremely variable, with no two individuals exactly alike, and females usually darker than males. Generally, the upperparts are grey-brown to grey, lighter on the head, and much chequered with white on the back, while the white-tipped tail is usually alternately barred

light and dark. The underparts are white, with dark brown spots, increasing in size and number towards the tail. The eye is dark brown, and the powerful legs and feet are yellow. Plumage variants range from almost unmarked white, to an all-over deep charcoal-brown, but the bird's size and powerful build should confirm its identity. Paler forms are predominant in the north of its range.

Habitat: The wild, remote Arctic mountains and wastelands are the usual habitat of this species, although it may occasionally occur in lightly wooded areas along the northern limit of the tree-line.

Nest: Gyr Falcons build no nest: the eggs are usually laid on an overhung cliff-ledge, but the birds will also use old nests of Rough-legged Buzzards and Ravens, even when these are in trees.

Food: This powerful predator feeds mainly on birds, ranging in size from small songbirds to geese. Ptarmigan form the greater part of its diet, although in some areas seabirds are taken in large numbers, while small mammals become more important in its winter quarters.

Range: The Gyr Falcon is distributed all around the Arctic, central Norway being its southernmost breeding limit in Europe.

Movements: Although some birds remain on their breeding grounds throughout the year, many (mostly immatures) move further south for the winter, though few go further south than Scandinavia and the northern USSR. Migration is more extensive in years with low numbers of Arctic gamebirds.

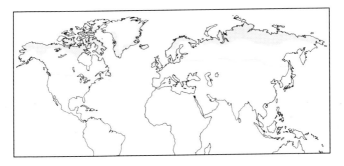

Peregrine Falcon
Falco peregrinus

Length:	35-48cm	**Eggs:**	2-5 (6), creamy, heavily marked red-brown
Wing:	267-381mm		
Weight ♂:	582-750g	**Incubation:**	28-29 days
Weight ♀:	925-1300g	**Fledging:**	35-42 days

Identification: The upperparts are dark slaty-blue, becoming almost black on the head where the darker colour extends down the sides to form a 'helmet'. The underparts are white on the chin, becoming gradually darker buff towards the tail, and becoming more heavily spotted and barred with black in the same direction. The tail is barred alternately blue-grey and black, with a dirty-white tip. The legs and feet are bright

yellow. The female is often darker, with pear-shaped spots on the breast, and heavier barring. There is considerable variation in size and colour, the species becoming gradually smaller and darker from north to south of its range, although it is always easily identified.

Habitat: Although the Peregrine Falcon is associated mainly with cliffs and rocky crags, most commonly along coasts, it is also found in both forested and open country, including grasslands and moorland, up to at least 3000 metres.

Nest: The most usual nest site is an inaccessible rocky ledge or hole, with a slight scrape being made for the eggs. Uncommon alternatives are the disused stick nest of some other species on a cliff or in a tree, a hollow tree-trunk or limb, or even a ledge on a tall building.

Food: The species preys almost exclusively on birds, ranging in size from small passerines up to wild duck, with pigeons (Columbidae) being specially favoured, but a few mammals, amphibians and even insects are also taken.

Range: Breeding areas include Scandinavia and northern USSR, with more scattered groups in other parts of Europe. The most widely distributed of all raptor species, the Peregrine Falcon has nevertheless given much cause for concern in recent decades due to rapid population declines in many areas caused by pesticides. Control of these chemicals has been followed by recovery in some places such as Britain.

Movements: Northern breeders are completely migratory, some travelling to the Mediterranean and Middle East. Southerly populations are more sedentary.

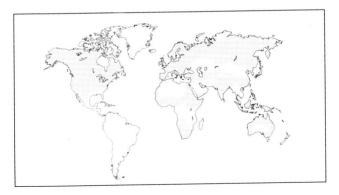

Index

RSNC

The Royal Society for Nature Conservation is pleased to endorse these excellent, fully illustrated pocket guide books which provide invaluable information on the wildlife of Britain and Europe. Royalties from each book sold will go to help the RSNC's network of 48 Wildlife Trusts and over 50 Urban Wildlife Groups, all working to protect rare and endangered wildlife and threatened habitats. The RSNC and the Wildlife Trusts have a combined membership of 184,000 and look after over 1800 nature reserves. If you would like to find out more, please contact RSNC, The Green, Whitham Park, Lincoln LN5 7NR. Telephone 0522 752326.